Totally Grown & Awesome™
Body
Facts
& Jokes

Published in MMXVIII by
Scribo, an imprint of
The Salariya Book Company Ltd
25 Marlborough Place, Brighton BN1 1UB
www.salariya.com

ISBN: 978-1-912233-63-2

SCRIBO   BOOK HOUSE   SCRIBBLERS

1 3 5 7 9 8 6 4 2

A CIP catalogue record for this book is available
from the British Library.

Printed and bound in China.
Printed on paper from sustainable sources.

Created and designed by
David Salariya.

Visit
www.salariya.com
for our online catalogue and
free fun stuff.

PAPER FROM
SUSTAINABLE
FORESTS

Author:
John Townsend worked as a
secondary school teacher before
becoming a full-time writer.
He specializes in illuminating and
humorous information books for
all ages.

Artist:
David Antram studied at
Eastbourne College of Art in
England and then worked in
advertizing before becoming a full-
time artist. He has illustrated many
children's non-fiction books.

Totally Gross & Awesome™

Body

Facts & Jokes

This Totally Gross & Awesome book belongs to:

....

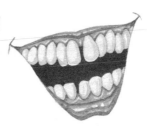

Written by

John Townsend

Illustrated by

David Antram

SCRIBO
a SALARIYA *imprint*

IntroduCtion

Warning—reading this book might not make you LOL (laugh out loud) but it could make you GOL (groan out loud), feel sick out loud, or SEL (scream even louder). If you're reading this in a library by a SILENCE sign… get ready to be thrown out for LOL-GOL-SEL!

The author really hasn't made anything up in this book (apart from some silly limericks and jokes).

He checked out the foul facts as best he could and even double-checked the fouler bits to make absolutely sure—so please don't get too upset if you find out something different or meet a world famous mad scientist/historian/total genius who happens to know better.

If I had my way, I'd RATify the lot!

5

Body Secrets

Your body is totally, amazingly, incredibly, mind-bogglingly, astoundingly EXCELLENT (most of the time). You're a miracle, a wonder of nature and a super machine full of surprises. You're also revolting. At least, sometimes your body can be disgusting, gross, and FOUL. Only read on if you want to know yourself better... warts and all. You don't want to know all of this—but you won't be able to stop yourself finding out!

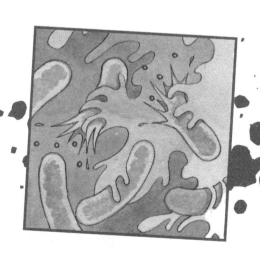

Body Boggling

Now here's the scary bit. You've got millions more cells than just your own. Only 1 in 10 of the cells in your body are human. So what are the other cells? They are made up of the incredible 90 trillion microbes that live on you or in you. They consist of bacteria, viruses, and other microorganisms. And it turns out that many of them play a vital role in keeping you healthy. You are crawling with life.

It's great to be alive... with bacteria!

To start off, you might be horrified to know that in the time it's taken you to read this far, you have lost thousands of cells that make up your body and brain. Millions of your cells die every minute. But don't panic—your body is making new cells all the time. Your body is packed with cells—in fact, scientists estimate there are over 37 trillion cells in the human body (give or take a few million). In one tiny drop of blood you have 5 million red cells and 15,000 white cells. There are 50 billion fat cells in the average body, and 2 billion heart muscle cells. So if you want to know how many cells you've got exactly, you'd better start counting. By the time you finish, you'll have lost a few billion more and grown plenty of new ones. The dead cells fall off, get absorbed and recycled by other cells or are pooped out of the body—gone and forgotten.

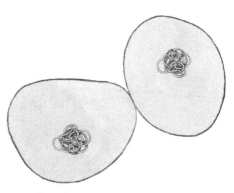

Not all bacteria are healthy— like those in a limerick...

On a toe sat a little bacterium
With millions of friends—but none queried 'em...
So they multiplied quickly
Till the host became sickly
With infection, much pus, and delirium.
(Just as well some antibiotics did the trick!)

And now for a joke about nasty body bacteria... Hmmm, maybe not—you might spread it.

ACHooo!

9

A Cheesy Doctor Sketch

Patient: Doctor, you've got to help me. It's my foot.

Doctor: Your foot? What do you mean?

Patient: It's that thing on the end of my leg.

Doctor: That's your bottom. Everyone has a bottom at the top.

Patient: No—the other end. It's my foot on the bottom.

Doctor: You've got a foot on your bottom or a bottom on your foot?

Patient: No—down there on the floor—that foot, on the end of my leg.

Doctor: What's wrong with it?

Patient: It's foul and cheesy.

Doctor: Is it just the one foot?

Patient: No, I've got two of them. They're both on the end of my legs. One on each.

Doctor: Are they the same?

Patient: No. One's right and one's left. My right leg is shorter than my left.

Doctor: Is that a problem for you?

Patient: Not really. I live on a slope.

Doctor: You'd better take off your boot so I can take a look.

Patient: Even though I've got a short right leg, it's amazing how my body has adjusted. My left leg is longer to make up for it.

Doctor: I can't help noticing you've got jelly in one ear and custard in the other.

Patient: Can you speak up a bit? I'm a trifle deaf.

11

Doctor: And you've got a sponge finger up your nose. I can tell what's wrong with you immediately.

Patient: What is it, doctor?

Doctor: You're not eating properly. And now that I can see your foot, I can tell you're not washing properly, either.

Patient: Washing? Why would I want to wash my left foot? I can't reach that one.

Doctor: But it's foul. It looks like foot rot—full of festering blue cheese.

Patient: Ah—so that's where my blue cheese and mayonnaise sandwich went. It fell in my boot.

Doctor: I think it's worse than that. It's full of bacteria.

Patient: No, that's ketchup. You can have a bite if you like.

Doctor: It stinks. I tell you, you've got foot rot.

Patient: I demand a second opinion.

Doctor: Certainly. You're crazy as well.

Patient: So what are you writing on your pad?

Doctor: It's a prescription.

Patient: What for?

Doctor: A bath. Goodbye. Next!

Why are some feet like the jokes in this book? They're as foul as foot rot and as cheesy as a cheddar factory!

More on Body Visitors

The average human foot contains more than **250,000** sweat glands, thousands more than in the armpits. They ooze a lovely soup of salts, sugars, and acids that provide a delicious feast for a colony of bacteria. In return for a free lunch, bacteria leave us with a cocktail of fatty acids that can give off that cheesy feet odor.

If you think your feet have lots of bacteria on them (millions between the toes and on the soles), your mouth is an action-packed bacteria theme park. Read on if you dare...

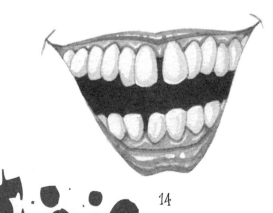

14

Bacteria in your mouth come in all shapes and sizes—with more of them than the whole world's human population. In fact, you've just swallowed a few million bacteria while reading this. Some types of bacteria live on your teeth, others prefer your gums, and others love the little cracks in your tongue. They happily swim in your spit (saliva) and paddle in your dribble. And while on that subject—did you know your mouth churns out half a gallon (about 2 liters) of saliva each day? In a lifetime you'd fill a good-sized swimming pool with your saliva. Quick tip—don't try to swim in it!

With all those fizzing, bubbling bacteria in your mouth, it's not surprising that tooth decay is common. It's caused by sticky deposits called plaque that coat gums and teeth. Plaque is made of bits of food, saliva, and bacteria that dissolve the enamel coating on each tooth and can gnaw away to the inside. So get brushing.

Body Cells Limerick

All your brain's cells, your body's and your heart's
Renew in unseen fits and starts.
There's division, formation,
And multiplication...
You're a wonderful sum of your parts!

Yet More Body Invaders

Unlike bacteria that are happy doing their own thing by themselves, a virus can only live inside one of your living cells. A virus takes over a cell and can cause disease by invading your body. There are many sorts of cold and flu viruses ready to invade, but your amazing immune system deals with millions of viruses and harmful bacteria each day. Your cells produce chemicals called antibodies that latch onto a virus and give it a good kicking.

Flu Jokes

I opened a window and in flew Enza (influenza).

Hmm—the jokes get better (but not much)

Did you know humans can catch bird flu as well as swine flu? For bird flu you need tweetment and for swine flu you need oinkment.

Someone once said that if scientists ever find a vaccination for influenza, pigs would fly. Sure enough, within a few days of a vaccine... swine flew (swine flu).

A woman walks into a doctor's office and sneezes, "Doctor, I feel terribly sick."
The doctor looks at her and asks, "Flu?"
"No," she says, "I came here on the bus."

Not everyone NOSE about sneezes

When you sneeze, tiny droplets from your mouth and nose fly through the air—possibly up to 100 miles an hour. Splashes can land up to 30 feet away, with bacteria and viruses flying in all directions. So if you feel a sneeze coming—reach for a handkerchief to help catch all those foul germs. It's sneezily done.

While on the subject of noses and what comes out of them—a word about snot (mucus). This slimy fluid in your nostrils stops dust, pollen, and dirt getting into your lungs and harming your breathing. When you breathe dry air into your nose, the mucus dries to form little clumps (boogers). You may have seen young kids picking their noses and eating boogers. Gross! If you think that's foul—you do much the same. You naturally swallow well over a mugful of nasal mucus every day—more when you've got a cold. Yuck!

19

Q: What's the difference between big green boogers and big green broccoli?
A: You can't get kids to eat broccoli.

If noses are for smelling and feet are for running, why do noses run and feet smell?

Q: What sound does a nut make when it sneezes?
A: Cashew

Which of these statements is true?

1. Every time you sneeze you kill thousands of brain cells.
2. When you sneeze your heart stops.
3. If you sneeze over 13 times at once, you will probably die.

Answer: They are all false

Yikes—I've just sneezed my brain into my tissue.

A Sneezy Tongue-Twister

If your nose freezes and teases in breezes
And your wheezes increases your sneezes,
Your snotty germ splutter
In the fridge on the butter...
Squeezes diseases on cheeses and displeases!

(In other words... keep your mucus to yourself)

Don't blame me for sneezing in the fridge. It's a tissue of lies (and germs!)

Another Cheesy Sneezy Doctor Sketch

Patient: Doctor, you've got to help me.

Doctor: Oh, it's you again. What's the matter this time?

Patient: I'm very stressed. I've just come back from a terrible camping trip.

Doctor: Little tense?

Patient: Yes—no room to stand up in them.

Doctor: How did you sleep?

Patient: Mainly with my eyes shut. One night I swallowed my sleeping bag.

Doctor: I thought you looked a bit down in the mouth. How did that happen?

Patient: In my dream I was eating a giant marshmallow and in the morning the pillow and sleeping bag had gone.

Doctor: Surely not. I find that hard to swallow.

Patient: I didn't.

Doctor: Go over to my window, stick your tongue out, and say "aaaaaah."

Patient: How will that help?

Doctor: You'll help scare the birds off my cherry tree. They're such a nuisance.

Patient: I've also got a sore knee—can you take a look?

Doctor: Mmm—you might have to go to the hospital.

Patient: Really? What is it?

Doctor: It's a building with doctors and nurses.

Patient: No—what is it that's wrong with my knee?

Doctor: It might need stretching.

Patient: Will it hurt?

Doctor: I'm only pulling your leg.

Patient: I find it painful when I kneel down.

Doctor: Well don't then.

Patient: (Squatting on hands and knees) You see?
Can you tell what's wrong?

I think you kneed a break.

Doctor: Now crawl over to the corner.

Patient: Ouch, this hurts.

Doctor: Can you pick up any fluff on the carpet while you're down there?

Patient: Never mind about the carpet. What about my knee?

Doctor: Turn round and crawl toward me.

Patient: Over here? Does that help?

Doctor: Hmm—not really. Now crawl into the middle of the room.

Patient: How is this helping you see what's wrong with me?

Doctor: It isn't. But this room needs a little table and I'm deciding where to put it.

Patient: This is absurd. I demand a second opinion.

Doctor: Very well—come back tomorrow and I'll have another look.

Patient: You're really getting up my nose (sneezes).

Doctor: It must be the dust from the carpet.

Patient: Quick—give me something for a sneezing fit, doctor.

Doctor: Very well. Take this.

Patient: Medicine?

Doctor: No—pepper. Goodbye. Next!

I've tested this mucus and the result is: It's SNOT very nice!

Stomach Churning
Horrors

Have you ever stopped to think about what you eat and what happens to it? Here's food for thought... In your lifetime, you'll eat over 35 tons of food (that's the weight of about 7 elephants). You'll probably poop out almost 3 elephants of poop in a lifetime. It's probably best not to do this all at once!

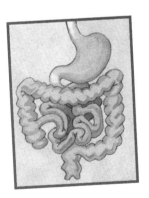

Your stomach contains strong hydrochloric acid to kill off bad bacteria and help you digest even the toughest pizza crusts. Your stomach's acid is strong enough to dissolve metal but it has no effect on plastic. Either way, it's not a good idea to swallow either.

It only takes seconds for your chewed-up food to reach your stomach, where it becomes a sloppy, churning liquid. As it gets pushed on through your intestines, the nutrients are absorbed into your bloodstream.

It takes about 12 hours to digest a meal completely. The leftover sludge and waste then get squeezed out through the colon and excreted from the body. Each day about 2.6 gallons of mashed up food and liquid goes through your body. Only a small amount ends up as poop.

Warning: GROSS ALERT

Apart from your stomach and intestines being alive with millions of microorganisms, they can also be home to tapeworms. These parasites can live in your gut for 20 years, growing more than 30 feet long, and you might not even know these creatures are there chomping away on your dinner.

A tapeworm is a wiggly, ribbon-shaped creature that lives inside people and animals, absorbing nutrients and laying millions of eggs.

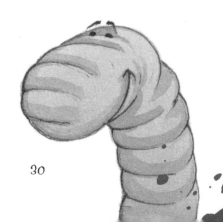

30

Despite the extreme "gross factor" of tapeworms, some people have apparently tried to swallow tapeworm eggs to help them lose weight and get slim. Maybe eating a little less and getting exercise is a better idea.

Don't worry about me – I'm just pulling a worm out of my arm.

Throughout history, vast numbers of the human race (children and adults) had worms inside their digestive systems. It is only with modern medicine and drugs that these worms have been controlled. Some scientists now think tapeworms may have been useful in controlling the body's immune systems. One theory is that when we started de-worming our bodies, it led to a rise in other diseases. Scary!

Gooey Innards

Digestion Riddle

Q: What punctuation mark can
be found in the body?

A: A colon (Your colon is part of your large
intestine and also a punctuation mark
like this : often used before a list.)

Did you know?

The gall bladder is a small
organ by your liver that
stores bile, which breaks
down the fat in your diet.

32

A very bad riddle

Q: If you see a small organ flying over the sea... what is it?

A: A gull bladder

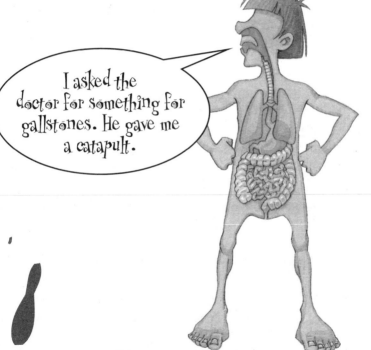

I asked the doctor for something for gallstones. He gave me a catapult.

A very bad pun

Is life going well? It depends on the liver. Doh!

You are what you eat

...silly limericks

The problem with poor Doctor Perkins
Was her passion for pickles and gherkins.
She swallowed too much
And perished from such,
By pickling her internal workings.

A woman from East of Kilbride
Ate ninety-six apples and died.
From over-indulging,
Her gut began bulging...
Brewing cider inside her insides.

If you eat too much spicy spaghetti
In high mountains you'll get very sweaty.
If you fail to ease off
And you suddenly cough,
You could end up lassoing a yeti.

Record Breakers

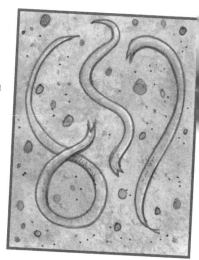

In 1990 a Japanese woman complained of severe stomach ache after eating raw fish. Doctors operated on her and removed 56 tiny wiggly worms from her stomach.

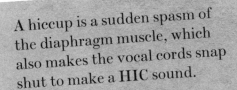

A hiccup is a sudden spasm of the diaphragm muscle, which also makes the vocal cords snap shut to make a **HIC** sound.

Why do we get hiccups? For a cheesy answer, take a look at the fable at the end of the book.

Are you ever troubled by horrible hiccups?

They don't usually last long—but not in the case of Charles Osborne (1894–1991) of Anthon, Iowa. He started hiccupping in 1922 while trying to weigh a pig, and couldn't stop. He was unable to find a cure and continued hiccupping until February 1990, a total of 68 years!

The pig had a bit of a hiccup, too.
He became bacon.

Rat 1: Digestion is awesome, you know. Hic!

Rat 2: That's true. Gnawing is never boring. If so, I'll eat my words.

Rat 1: You're always eating everything. Hic!

Rat 2: Yeah—I'm a rat. It's my job.

Rat 1: A fat rat, too. You ought to go on a diet. Hic!

Rat 2: So should you. It might stop your hiccups.

Rat 1: Don't be silly. Rats don't get hiccups. Hic!

Rat 2: Anyway, I am on a diet. It's called the sea food diet.

My hiccups are out of control.

Rat 1: Why—do you only eat food from the sea?

Rat 2: Nah—whenever I SEE FOOD, I eat it.

Rat 1: Well I'm on the lettuce diet and I've lost a lot of weight.

Rat 2: Does that mean you only eat lettuce?

Rat 1: Nah. Whatever I want, I just say "LET-US eat it."

Rat 2: I can see a bit of lettuce sticking out of your nose right now.

Rat 1: That's only the tip of the iceberg. Hic!

Rat 2: Doh!

39

A Whiff of Trouble

While on the subject of digestion, a tricky topic cannot be avoided. We all make it and release it. Sometimes it can be embarrassing. Here's a clue...

"Doctor, doctor—can you give me something for gas?"

"Certainly, madam. I'll get you just the thing from my cupboard."

"That's good. I feel very embarrassed. What do you provide for constant wind?"

"This. It's a kite. And if you need anything more—try a yacht."

Most people release enough gas each day from burping and farting to fill a balloon. You're not always aware of "leaking gas" unless it makes a noise or smells. The average person "passes wind" about 12 times a day or more. It's actually a sign of a healthy digestive system—but you're advised not to do it too often in public.

Turn the page for some rip-roaring advice.

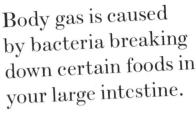

Body gas is caused
by bacteria breaking
down certain foods in
your large intestine.

Beans, bran, broccoli, brussel
sprouts, cabbage, cauliflower,
and onions are well-known for
fermenting inside you and giving
off nitrogen, carbon dioxide,
hydrogen, and methane.

Hydrogen sulfide is
particularly smelly—like
rotten eggs. All these high-
fiber foods are good for you
but also good for "wind"—
usually called flatulence.

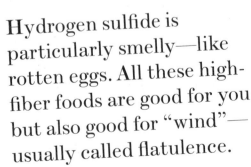

42

Psst—here's a foul secret you ought to know. If you fly on a plane, remember to keep a clothespin handy for popping on your nose mid-flight. The thing is (wait for it...) flying makes us fart more.

The change of air pressure causes bloating when small amounts of air inside us expand, and there's only one way it's going to get out. This can be a real problem for pilots. Maybe that's why some of them have strange looks on their faces and they walk a bit weirdly—but that's nothing compared to astronauts.

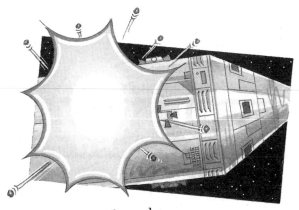

In fact, at one stage it was feared astronauts' flatulence would be lethal in the confines of a cabin. Scientists described the risk of a fireball exploding from the high concentration of human gas in a spacecraft. We have blast-off!

43

Here's a foul flatulence fact that made a French fortune. Brace yourself for a gross story.

A French entertainer named Joseph Pujol (1857–1945) was known as "Le Petomane" from the French word peter which means "to fart." Believe it or not, Pujol could control his abdominal muscles so well that he could break wind to music and play tunes from his rear end. He would even play the trombone from his bottom and his audiences would laugh so much that nurses had to be on hand to help anyone who fainted from laughing!

And now a tune from the wind section called "Odor Joy."

A Royal Trump (joke)

Queen Victoria was sitting elegantly
(side-saddle) on her favorite horse,
having just married Prince Albert.

As he rode up beside her, her horse
broke wind very violently, with an ear-
splitting rasp and eye-watering smell.

The queen smiled at her new husband,
"I do apologize about that, my dear."
"That's all right, your majesty," he answered.
"In fact, I quite thought it was your horse."

45

Foul, Cheesy, and Breezy

Your body has millions of parts,
Some gurgle in loud fits and starts
With crackles and pops,
Drips, sploshes, and plops,
Squelches, blasts, rumbles,
and f.... (foul noises!)

A windy limerick

An old woman steps into a Manhattan elevator when a pretty young woman enters behind her, smelling of expensive perfume. She turns to the old woman and says arrogantly, "Romance by Ralph Lauren, $300 an ounce."

Another young and beautiful woman enters the elevator, also smelling of expensive perfume. She announces to everyone, "My scent is Chanel Number 27 at $400 an ounce."

When the elevator stops, the old woman looks both women in the eye before bending over and breaking wind. She winks with a smile, "Lima beans, 75 cents a pound!"

Tales of the Heart

The average adult heart beats 72 times a minute; 100,000 times a day; 3,600,000 times a year; and 2.5 billion times during a lifetime. Beat that!

Because the heart has its own electrical impulse, it can actually keep beating even when separated from the body, as long as it has a good supply of oxygen. Please don't put this to the test!

Heart Riddle

Q: What has 13 hearts, but no other organs?
A: A deck of playing cards.

Groundbreaking

In 1929, the German surgeon Werner Forssmann (1904-1979) examined the inside of his own heart by threading a catheter into a vein in his arm and pushing it all the way into his heart. His high risk experiment helped him invent a new type of operation called cardiac catheterization, which is now a common procedure.

On December 3, 1967, Dr. Christiaan Barnard (1922-2001) of South Africa transplanted a human heart into the body of Louis Washansky. Although Louis lived only 18 days, this was considered the first successful heart transplant. Today about 3,500 heart transplants are performed each year around the world.

Your heart pumps blood with enough pressure to squirt it up to 30 feet in the air. (Please accept this as "about" 30 feet—as it really isn't a good idea to test this out.)

The human body has about 60,000 miles of blood vessels—long enough to stretch around the world at least twice. (Why would anyone want to do that?)

Although you can't survive without a beating heart, it's possible for your body to survive without some of its internal organs. Even if you lose your stomach, your spleen, 75 percent of your liver, 80 percent of your intestines, one kidney, one lung, and various other organs, you could carry on living (maybe not as well as before). If possible, it's a good idea to keep the lot!

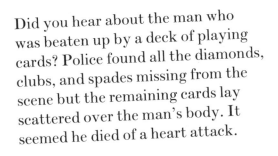

Did you hear about the man who was beaten up by a deck of playing cards? Police found all the diamonds, clubs, and spades missing from the scene but the remaining cards lay scattered over the man's body. It seemed he died of a heart attack.

Heart Joke

A man needs a heart transplant and his surgeon tells him the only heart available is from a sheep. The man agrees to have it so the surgeon transplants the sheep's heart into the man. A few days after the operation, the surgeon gives the patient a checkup and asks, "How are you feeling?"

The man replies, "Not BAAAAD!", pulls on a thick woollen sweater, and skips off across the fields.

Body Quiz

Here are some three letter words to describe the not-so-nice parts of the body: yuk, eek, and ugh. But can you name 10 parts of the human body that have only 3 letters?

When you've got a list, turn to page 113 for the answers.

....
....
....
....
....
....
....
....
....
....

51

Hairy, scary, icky, & sticky

Hair contains protein called keratin, which is the same material that makes up your fingernails, toenails, and teeth (as well as horns and hooves in animals).

So who's the hairiest?

You've got about 5 million hairs all over your body—apart from on the soles of your feet, the palms of your hands, and your lips. In fact, you've got as many hairs as a chimpanzee has—but yours are finer and lighter so they're hard to see. That's if you don't suffer from a rare hairy condition called hypertrichosis which makes body hair grow thickly all over—even all over the face (women as well). This is sometimes called "werewolf syndrome." Think of the cost at the hairdressers.

HOWWWL

53

5 Hairy Records

The longest human hair in the world measures more than 18 feet. Since the age of 13 in 1973, Xie Qiuping of China didn't cut her hair. After thirty years her hair was 18 feet, 5.5 inches (5.6 meters) long.

54

The longest mustache on record in 2010 measured 14 feet (4.3 meters) and belonged to Ram Singh Chauhan from India.

If the average man never shaved, his beard would reach 13 feet long in his 70s. In fact, the longest beard on record in 2011 measured 8 feet, 2.5 inches (2.4 m) and belonged to Sarwan Singh of Canada.

How about ear hair? A man from India named Radhakant Bajpai has hair sprouting from both ears that is over 5 inches (13 centimeters) long.

Really hairy legs might freak you out—but can you imagine leg hair nearly 4 inches (10 cm) long? Julian Rowe of the UK holds that record.

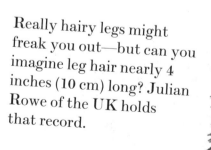

Hairy jokes

Did you hear about the man who lost all his hair in the war? He lost it in a hair raid.

"Doctor, doctor... all my hair is falling out. What can you give me to keep it in?"

"I've got a very nice paper bag. That should be ideal for keeping it in."

Hairy Limerick

There was an old lady called Mary
Whose face was exceptionally hairy.
She said, "It isn't so weird
That I've got a long beard...
It's my green furry body that's scary!"

Your hair can be home to extra life. Apart from head lice being a common problem, your eyelashes can be a great place for tiny mites that you can't see as they're so small. In fact, most humans have these tiny mites living in their eyelashes. They live in the hair follicles and pores of your face, and particularly love eyelashes, where they feed on oils and dead skin cells. Yum!

Yucky, Mucky, & Unlucky

1. Pus

Spots and cuts on your skin can become infected and ooze with pus—which is a white or yellowish fluid. It's a mix of decomposed body tissue, bacteria, and white blood cells that are fighting the infection. Sometimes the pores in your skin get blocked and infected, which can cause acne. Washing, rather than popping pimples, is best for unclogging those pores.

Spot the problem.

2. Sweat

Every day your skin leaks more than two pints (1 liter) of sweat. On hot days or if you run a lot, it will be much more (maybe 2.6 gallons). That's because you have sweat glands all over your body except on your ears, lips, and nails. On the palms of your hand and the soles of your feet, you have about 100 sweat glands per square inch. Altogether, females have more sweat glands than males, even though males tend to sweat more. It's your body's way of cooling you down. The only trouble is, bacteria love sweat and once they get to work on it, it starts to smell—so don't forget to wash under the arms especially.

3. Belly Button Fluff

Have you ever peered into your belly button and seen a clump of blue-gray fluff? Many people collect fluff (called lint) in their navels—a weird mix of clothing fibers, skin cells, bacteria, and all sorts. Not all of us collect fluff in our navels. Less hairy-bellied people will collect less lint, as it's the hairs around our belly buttons that channel the fluff into the depression. Fluff might actually help keep our belly buttons cleaner by collecting bacteria.

Believe it or not, an Australian man, Graham Barker, has saved a record-breaking 0.77 ounces (or 22.1 grams) of his belly button fluff after collecting it every day for 26 years. He keeps it all in labeled jars. He's a librarian but ought to be a navel officer!

4. Ear Wax

The oozy, yellow-brown, smelly, yucky stuff in your ears does a great job. It stops bad things getting into your head! Ear wax can be yellow, orange, dark brown, or even black and you tend to make more ear wax when you get stressed—like when you're reading this and worrying about your gunky ears. Just relax.

Eek, my head's leaking!

5. Eye Gunk

Do you sometimes wake up with your eyes gummed up and your eyelashes all crusty? Eye goo is actually good stuff— an oily fluid that keeps your eyelids blinking, stops bacteria harming your eyes, and prevents tears from constantly rolling down your cheeks. But sometimes, when you're asleep it can clog up the eyes—but a quick slosh of clean water usually does the trick. Blink and it's gone!

More Dopey Limericks

Your eyes are incredible features
Much better than some other creatures'
Unless, very sadly,
Your pupils fail badly…
Like those of incompetent teachers!

There was a young cyclist named Mike
Whose ear wax was not as he'd like.
It seeped out his ears
In thick yellow smears...
So he used it for oiling his bike.

My eyes, one blue and one green
Are the weirdest that anyone's seen.
They're at the back of my head,
So I can't see where I tread...
But at least I can tell where I've been.

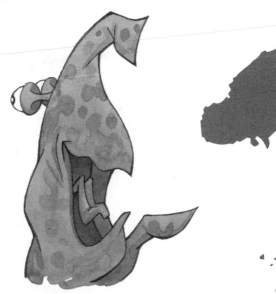

Random Records

Kim Goodman of Chicago can push out her eyeballs about half an inch (over a centimetre) beyond her eye sockets. Measuring an "eye pop" is an exact science that has to be done by an optometrist using a device known as a proptometer which accurately measures bulging eyes with an eyewatering reading. Kim must look like a startled chameleon that's stepped on a thorn.

What are you gawking at?

Sit and listen

In 2009, 27 year-old Julia Schwarz of Germany got into a fight with a friend, who bit off Julia's ear. Surgeons soon got to the bottom of her problem. Firstly they had to patch up her injured head but what could they do with her severed ear in the meantime? Simple—sew it on her behind. They made a small incision in her bottom and stitched the ear into the slit where it was kept "alive" until they were ready for a further operation. Her "rear ear" certainly made her sit up and listen!

Warts and all

Did you know...

Warts are small bumps on the skin that usually appear on people's hands or feet.

Warts are contagious and caused by a virus that enters the body through broken skin.

Between 10% and 20% of children get skin warts. Girls tend to get more warts than boys.

Many myths have spread about warts—like they can be caught by touching a toad. Although toads may look like they have contagious warts, they don't and do not spread them. Witches with warts on their nose are part of old folklore.

WART a fuss over nothing.

There are over 100 different types of the human wart virus, which is why warts are quite common.

Skin and Bones

Did you know you were born with 300 bones in your body but as you grow into an adult you'll have 206. That's not because you lose any, but because many join together. It's just as well really—without bones, you'd just be a heap of skin and organs splodged on the floor! In fact, your skin is your biggest organ and it holds you together. Without it, you'd be a gooey mess. An adult's skin could stretch out to the size of a large blanket.

Don't forget that your skin is constantly shedding cells. Most of the dust you see is dead skin cells (like under your bed). In your lifetime, you're likely to shed about 40 pounds (19 kilograms) of skin— the weight of five gallons of milk. How gross is that? Not as gross as what's coming next...

Right now there could be over a million little creatures in your bed chomping away on your dead skin cells. You share your bed with microscopic dust mites that feed off the skin cells that fall off you in the night. Delicious!

There's nothing quite like breakfast in bed.

Did you know?

The average human body contains enough bones to make an entire human skeleton. Doh!

Doh!

Biology

Teacher: The kidneys are important organs of the body. What is a kid-ney?

Student: That's easy. It's the name of that joint halfway down a child's leg.

74

And now for the oldest cheesy riddle in the book:

Q: Why didn't the skeleton go to the party?

A: He had no body to go with. Groan.

What a rib-tickling, side-splitting joke!

Yet Another Cheesy Doctor Skit

Patient: Doctor, you've got to help me.

Doctor: Oh, it's you again. What's the matter this time?

Patient: I'm all itchy. Can you cure me?

Doctor: I never give rash promises.

Patient: But that's not all, doctor. When I press my leg it hurts. Then when I press my chest it hurts. When I press my head it hurts. When I press my stomach it hurts. If I stop pressing, I get upset. What's wrong with me?

Doctor: Well, that's obvious—for a start you must have a sore finger. And when you stop pressing, you're de-pressing yourself. How's your heart?

Patient: To be honest, doctor—I'm sure I have a hole in my heart. I woke up in the night and felt it here in my chest. Can you take a close look?

Doctor: Let me see...

Patient: Here—you can feel it.

Doctor: No—that's your wedding ring in your top pocket. You should just go home and forget it.

Patient: Forget what?

Doctor: Ah, that could be it—amnesia.

Patient: I've never been to Amnesia and I've never met an Amnesian.

Doctor: To be honest, I've got no idea what's wrong with you. It could be down to stress.

Patient: In that case, I'll come back when you're more relaxed.

77

Doctor: Not me—you! Are you sleeping well?

Patient: Not really. Last night I slept on the roof. It took me ages to drop off. Mind you, I snore so loudly that I keep myself awake at night.

Doctor: Then I suggest you sleep in another room to give yourself a break.

Patient: I always have a mug of cocoa at bedtime to help me sleep.

Doctor: Does that help?

Patient: Not really. Every time I drink it I get a terrible pain in my eye.

Doctor: Try taking the spoon out of the mug.

Patient: I hadn't thought of that. Mind you, when I get up in the morning I feel really bad for an hour and then I'm fine.

Doctor: Try getting up an hour later, then.

Patient: That won't work. As soon as I get out of bed I go all weird and wobbly.

Doctor: Weird and wobbly? How do you mean?

Patient: I see things all around me and feel faint.

Doctor: You see things all around you? Like what?

Patient: Mickey Mouse, Donald Duck, Goofy, The Jungle Book....

Doctor: Hmmm, you're having nasty Disney spells. Here, take these...

Patient: Pills?

Doctor: No—DVDs. The BFG and Zootopia. Goodbye. Next!

You've got heartburn from eating too much birthday cake... with the candles burning.

Did you know...

25 percent of all your bones are in your feet: there are 26 bones in each foot, many very small.

When you take one step, you are using up to **200** muscles. Brisk walking uses plenty of muscle power and is a great way to exercise. It's cheaper than the gym, too!

It takes more muscles to frown than to smile: Scientists can't agree on the exact number, but many more muscles are required to make you look miserable. So SMILE!

Your tongue is the strongest muscle in your body, compared to its size. You may not use it to lift weights but think of all the exercise it gets when you gossip.

Not for the squeamish...

Dead Bodies

Did you know?

People used to buy and sell dead human bodies. There was much money to be made in the 1700s and 1800s from the sale of fresh corpses. As the study of anatomy increased in Europe there was a demand for bodies to study in universities and hospitals. In winter, when medical schools were in session and corpses in graveyards were better preserved by the cold, body-snatchers went on the prowl. Grave-robbers would enter churchyards in the dead of night to dig up fresh corpses—the fresher, the better.

The risk of having a body snatched was greater for the poor. Richer people could afford more secure graves with an iron cage, stone vaults, or guards, to protect their dead relatives. Don't have nightmares...

Do you want to read a really good body-snatcher joke?

Maybe not—you might die laughing and get carried away.

Some Killer Facts

Brain cells die within a few minutes of the heart stopping. Skin cells can survive for up to 24 hours.

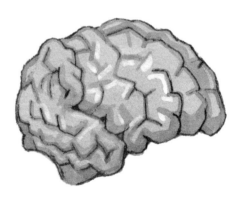

Dead bodies swell up like balloons after about four days, due to the gases and liquids gurgling inside.

It sometimes appears as if fingernails and toenails continue to grow after death. They don't—but as the skin dries and contracts around them, it looks as if they have grown.

Live
Gruesome Stuff

Is it possible for a living person's body to burst into flames for no apparent reason?

For well over **100** years there have been reports of people suddenly and mysteriously exploding in a ball of fire. Known as spontaneous human combustion, this has been described in many popular books on the unexplained and in fiction.

Although there is little scientific evidence to prove that people can suddenly "ignite from within," some victims have burned to death in their own homes. For some reason, nothing else around them burns and all that remains is a pile of human ashes and maybe a shoe. So next time you feel as if you're burning with rage... watch out!

Grave Tales

Here lies the body of Great Aunt Anna,
Done to death by a banana.
It wasn't the fruit that actually killed her
But the slippery skin and Cousin Matilda.

Everyone knows that dead Egyptian pharaohs were turned into mummies. But did you know that meant scrubbing down the body and removing all the internal organs apart from the heart? Then the body was stuffed and the brain was mashed up and pulled out through the nose. Everything was dried out before being wrapped up in cloth strips. And what sort of special Egyptian doctor would perform this task? A Cairo-practor, of course. (That last bit is just a cheesy joke and shouldn't be written in an exam or you won't get tomb-any marks, pharaoh enough?)

Brainy stuff

Your brain is mind-boggling! It sends electric pulses throughout your body, with enough power to keep a light bulb blazing. Your brain burns up 20 percent of the energy from the food you eat. This wrinkly, squelchy, dense organ needs oxygen and water to keep it alive. Starved of oxygen for only a few minutes, the human brain will be damaged beyond repair. As 80 percent of your brain is water, it's important to keep properly hydrated for the sake of your mind: Think **DRINK!**

Time for a quick brainwash.

92

You might think that your brain is more active during the day when the rest of your body is moving around. But it isn't. Your brain is more active when you sleep. It comes out to play at night, as you'll soon find out when you come to the weird stuff about sleep and dreams.

No Brainer

Although your brain is very delicate and has to be protected by a strong skull, there are amazing stories of people surviving the most horrific head injuries.

One of the most famous survivors of a hole in the brain was Phineas Gage of Cavendish, Vermont. Phineas was a 25 year-old railroad worker in 1848, when he was packing explosives that suddenly went off. An iron rod flew up and went right through his left cheek. It pushed through his skull and came out the top of his head.

94

Amazingly, Phineas wasn't knocked out and he remained awake but a bit confused while he was operated on by doctors. In fact, he lived for another 12 years despite his terrible brain injury.

Phineas changed from being a hard-working foreman to a gruff, bad-tempered man.

These changes in his personality gave scientists useful information about how the front parts of the brain work. We now know the area called the frontal lobe controls our moods but you use it every day to make decisions, such as what to eat or drink, as well as for thinking or studying. The frontal lobe is also where our personality is formed and where we can carry out higher mental processes such as planning and speaking fluently.

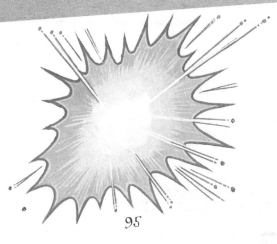

Brainy Jokes

What does a brain do when it sees a friend across the street?

It has a quick brain wave.

My brain surgeon was very rude to me so I decided to give him a piece of my mind. He then suggested he could clone a new brain for me, but I was in two minds about it. In the end I decided I was getting a head of myself.

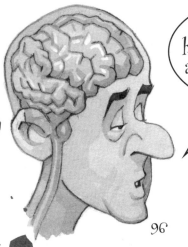

I was about to have a brain transplant and changed my mind.

96

Brainy Limericks

See your face—and what could be cuter?
Just behind it, your brain's a sharpshooter
By firing like lightning,
Its power is frightening…
More advanced than any computer.

It's a wonderful thinking machine
With its magical secrets unseen.
But there it resides,
With an ear on both sides
And that wonder of science in between!

Your brain is so strangely designed
With neurons and crinkles combined.
It takes mighty brains
To think what it contains
Imagine how it's all in the mind!

Sleepy Slumbers & Neurotic Nightmares

Are you feeling tired? Maybe you're tired of feeling foul and cheesy. If you're tired and thinking of going to sleep—be warned...

Humans spend a third of their entire lives sleeping. By the age of 75, the average person has spent 25 years zonked out, 6 years dreaming, and probably almost 30 years in bed. That could mean a lot of lying around with creepy crawlies!

Have you heard the scary report about what you swallow in your sleep? The average person, it is claimed, swallows eight spiders a year while they are fast asleep so they don't even know about it. Are you horrified? Don't lose sleep over it—it's all a silly myth. Mind you... there's no telling how many bed bugs might be crawling over you when you sleep. There again, you might sleep on your feet as you go for a stroll...

I spy with my little eyes...

Sleepwalking

It's thought that 15 to 18 percent of the population are sleepwalkers from time to time. It tends to affect children ages 6 to 12 mostly, with boys more likely to sleepwalk than girls. Sleepwalking seems to run (or walk) in families, and a "walkabout" in the night could last from a few seconds to over half an hour. The funny thing is, you won't know you've been sleepwalking unless someone wakes you up in the middle of the night. Don't worry—it's a myth that it's dangerous to wake someone who is sleepwalking. So relax... and lie down (if you dare!)

Believe it or not, some people have done bizarre things in their sleep. Some sleepwalkers start eating, gardening, writing e-mails, or get dressed, leave the house, and even drive a car (presumably their own). Usually, when sleepwalkers wake up, they have no memory of what they did, even though their eyes were open. Scary.

ZZZZZZZz

3 True Stories to Keep You Awake

1. In 1987, Kenneth Parks of Toronto, Canada, got out of bed while he was still asleep, drove to his parents-in-laws' home, and murdered his mother-in-law. His father-in-law was very lucky to escape. When he woke up later, Kenneth was horrified to discover blood all over his hands, so he called the police. After a long investigation, the police consulted psychiatrists and many sleep specialists. Eventually, Kenneth was found innocent of murder because he could not be held responsible for his actions. His crime was given the grand title of "homicidal somnambulism." That's murder while you're asleep. Please don't try it.

2. In 2005, a 15 year-old girl in London got up in the night and went sleepwalking through town. For some bizarre reason, she headed toward a high crane and began to climb it. When someone saw her fast asleep on the arm of the crane 12 stories above a construction site, they called the emergency services. The rescue took two hours: waking her suddenly could cause the girl to panic and fall. She was eventually carried off the crane, brought down in an elevator, and taken to the hospital to be checked. She was fine so was sent home... back to a comfy bed.

3. Just imagine being woken up by the taste of salt and grit in your mouth—then to find you're in the sea. In 2015, a woman in the UK did just that and suddenly woke up in the sea after walking half a mile in her sleep at 1:30 in the morning. She'd climbed down steps and over rocks before wading into the waves. Luckily a porter at a nearby hotel saw her and went to her rescue. The sleepwalker almost became a sleep-swimmer—but fortunately arrived back home safe and unharmed (although a bit damp).

Scary Sleep

Some people can be sound asleep on their backs and suddenly wake up but their body is in "lock-down." It's as if they're frozen and can't move or speak. This is known as "sleep paralysis," and can last from a few seconds to minutes, so it can cause real panic. It is still a mystery why this happens to many sleepers at some point in their lives. In fact, the science of human sleep and how it affects our bodies and minds is still full of secrets.

Q. Did you hear about the man who slept under an old tractor?
A. He wanted to wake up oily in the morning.

Sleepy Jokes

When she woke up from a vivid dream, a woman told her husband,

"I just dreamed that you gave me a pearl necklace for our anniversary. What do you think it means?"

"You'll know tonight," he said.

That evening, the man came home with a small package and gave it to his wife.

"Dreams really can come true!" she squealed with delight, as she hurriedly opened it to find... a book entitled "The Meaning of Dreams." Doh!

Did you hear about the boy who slept with his head under the pillow? When he woke up, he discovered the fairies had taken out all his teeth!

Final Doctor Jokes

"Doctor, doctor, after the operation on my hand, will I be able to be a world-famous pianist?"
"Of course."
"That's good, because I can't play the piano."

"Doctor, doctor, I keep thinking I'm a dog."
"Lie down on the couch and I'll examine you."
"I can't, I'm not allowed on the furniture."

"Doctor, doctor, I keep thinking
I've turned into a moth!"
"You need a psychiatrist—why
did you come to see me?"
"Your light was on."

And Finally...

By now, you will know your body is truly amazing (as well as occasionally foul and cheesy). Despite all the things that can go wrong with our bodies, today we have the wonders of modern science to put us right. In the past, it was bad news if your body became infected, if you caught disease or even plague. At one time, if your body became poisoned and a limb turned black with gangrene, there was no choice but to have it sawn off while all you could do was scream.

Aaah it's the expensive plague doctor with his huge bill!

Don't have nightmares too much—and may your body and mind relax after this dip into the truly foul and cheesy world that is **YOU!** Watch for other books in this series to find out more revolting, yucky, disgusting groan-out-loud facts and jokes... if your stomach is strong enough. Speaking of stomachs...

An Aesop Fable as a Bedtime Story...

Long ago, the parts of the human body did not work together as well as they do today. Each part had its own opinion and was determined to speak. They were all cross with the stomach, which just sat there getting full while everyone else had to do all the work.

Eventually, all parts of the body decided to go on strike to make the stomach see sense. The hands refused to bring food to the mouth, the teeth refused to chew, and the throat refused to swallow anything. In their effort to make the stomach go hungry, the various parts of the body soon began to feel weak until the whole body started to waste away. Soon they all realized that the work done by the stomach was really important and that the food it consumed was shared with everyone else. The nourishment it provided allowed all to flourish and thrive, since the stomach enriched the blood, providing life to all.

Since that time, all the parts of the body now get along just fine. Mind you, now and again, you might notice the stomach has a little grumble just to let the rest of the body remember that everyone needs everyone else. So next time you have the hiccups, just relax— it's your stomach having a little giggle about a particular matter from long ago. Hic!

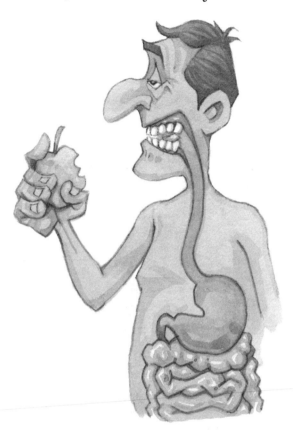

Body Quiz answers
(from page 51)

1. Leg   2. Arm   3. Eye   4. Toe   5. Hip

6. Rib   7. Jaw   8. Gum   9. Ear   10. Lip

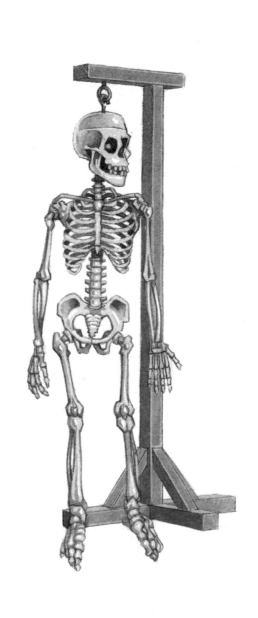

QUIZ

1. What is the main cause of tooth decay?

a) Plaque

b) The dentist

c) Talking to your friends

2. What causes smelly feet?

a) Eating too much cheese

b) Bacteria

c) Extremely fluffy socks

3. Where do tapeworms usually live?

a) In the earth

b) Inside animals

c) Under the kitchen sink

4. What is the digestive sytem for?

a) It keeps our arms and legs moving

b) It helps us breathe underwater

c) It breaks down food

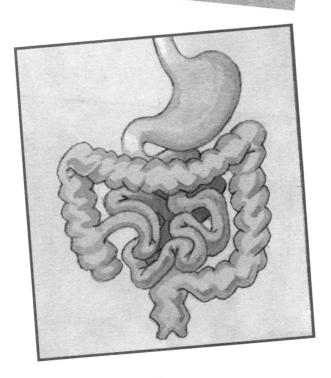

5. If you pass wind regularly, it is often a sign that...

a) You have a healthy digestive system

b) It is good weather to fly a kite

c) You should see a doctor

6. After we've eaten our food, most of it gets absorbed. What happens to the rest?

a) It explodes

b) It is used to make our brains bigger

c) It gets excreted out as poop

7. We all have tiny mites living in our eyelashes. What do they like to eat?

a) Oils and dead skin cells

b) Boogers and ear wax

c) Chips and chocolate

8. Why do our ears produce ear wax?

a) For cyclists to oil their bikes

b) To stop our brains from running out of our ears

c) To stop dirt getting into our heads

9. What is another
name for snot?

a) Mucus

b) Slime

c) Wax

SNIFF!

10. How do people catch warts?

a) By touching a toad

b) By a virus

c) By being near a witch

11. The brain needs oxygen to keep alive. What else does it need?

a) Water

b) Pizza

c) Heavy rock music

12. How many bones does an adult have?

a) 300

b) 206

c) Almost enough to make a skeleton

13. What is the farthest that the blood vessels in a human body can stretch?

a) Across a football field

b) At least twice around the world

c) Over a double bed

14. What causes body gas?

a) Bacteria breaking down certain foods in our large intestine

b) Watching too much TV

c) Forgetting to brush your teeth

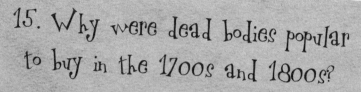

15. Why were dead bodies popular to buy in the 1700s and 1800s?

a) They were used in puppet shows

b) They were used to study anatomy in colleges and hospitals

c) They were used as artwork

Answers:

1 = a
2 = b
3 = b
4 = c
5 = a
6 = c
7 = a
8 = c

9 = a
10 = b
11 = a
12 = b
13 = b
14 = a
15 = b

GLOSSARY

Bacteria: microscopic lifeforms, which are usually single-celled and often cause disease.

Brain: the gray organ in your head that allows you to think, feel, and act.

Catheter: a tube inserted into an opening in the body to remove fluids.

Neurons: a type of cell in the body, especially the brain, that transmits electrical and chemical signals, allowing us to think, move, and feel.

Pore: a very small opening in the skin through which liquids, gases, or microscopic particles can pass.

Pupils: the dark opening in the center of the eye through which light passes.

Vaccination: the process by which a person is exposed to a small sample of a disease so that their immune system can develop the ability to deal with the real thing.

Virus: a microscopic lifeform that infects another organism, multiplies itself, and causes illness.

INDEX

I finished reading this Totally Gross & Awesome book on:

........../........../..........